382

k is to be returned on or before

Johann Gutenberg

by Michael Pollard

OTHER TITLES IN THE SERIES
Alexander Graham Bell by Michael Pollard (1-85015-200-4)
Charles Darwin by Anna Sproule (1-85015-213-6)
Thomas Edison by Anna Sproule (1-85015-201-2)
Albert Einstein by Fiona Macdonald (1-85015-253-5)
Alexander Fleming by Beverley Birch (1-85015-184-9)
Galileo Galilei by Michael White (1-85015-227-6)
Guglielmo Marconi by Beverley Birch (1-85015-185-7)
Margaret Mead by Michael Pollard (1-85015-228-4)
Isaac Newton by Michael White (1-85015-243-8)
James Watt by Anna Sproule (1-85015-254-3)
The Wright Brothers by Anna Sproule (1-85015-229-2)

Picture Credits:
Cover: Scala, Hulton Picture Company; Archiv Fur Kunst: 4, 10, 14, 30, 34, 50, 52; Christie's Colour Library: 45, 48; Exley Photo Library: 55; Explorer Archives: 9 (A Le Toquin), 16 (A Le Toquin), 23 (Bibl. Nat. Paris), 28, 29, 44 (Desmarteau), 49, 54 (Philip Roy); Hulton Picture Company: 7, 33, 38 (top), 43; R.T.H.P.L.: 39; Ronald Sheridan/Ancient Art & Architecture Collection: 5, 13, 27, 37; Ann Ronan Picture Library: 20, 46; Scala: 9, 12, 18, 18-9, 38, 40, 41; Science Photo Library: 51 (J.L. Charmet), 58 (top Malcolm Fielding, Johnson Matthey), 59 (Andrzej Dudzinski); Spectrum Colour Library: 58 (G Mitchell).

Thanks go to Ivor Powell of West Herts College
Department of Printing and Packaging.

Published in Great Britain in 1992
by Exley Publications Ltd,
16 Chalk Hill, Watford,
Herts WD1 4BN, United Kingdom.

ISBN 1-85015-255-1

Series editor: Helen Exley.
Picture editor: Alex Goldberg.
Editorial: Samantha Armstrong.
Typeset by Brush Off Studios,
St Albans.
Printed and bound in Hungary.

Johann Gutenberg

*The story of the invention of movable type
and how printing led to a knowledge explosion*

Michael Pollard

Suspense

Johann Gutenberg, printer, paced up and down his room in Mainz, Germany. Now and again, he went to the window and looked along the street. Once or twice he thought he heard footsteps outside, and stopped to listen. But the sound passed by.

It was a late afternoon in November 1455. Several hours earlier, Gutenberg had sent two of his workmen, Heinrich Keffer and Bechtolf von Hanau, to the Mainz city court. There, a case was being heard against Gutenberg and he could not bear to go himself. It was more than he could stomach to sit in court waiting for the decision to be made – a decision which could mean that everything he had worked for for over twenty years was in ruins. So he had sent the two men to bring back the news.

As he waited, Gutenberg thought back over the years. He remembered how, as a young man, he had had the first thrill of an idea that could change the world. He thought of the long hours of work late into the night, the disappointments and delays when things went wrong, constant worries about money. And now, in his mid-fifties, just as things were coming right and he was beginning to have something to show for his years of hard work, he looked like losing everything.

At last, the two workmen came back. He could tell from the way they kept their heads bent, avoiding his eyes, that they had not brought good news.

"So it is over?" he said.

The two men nodded.

"Have I anything left?"

"Nothing," said Heinrich Keffer. "Johann Fust wins everything – the business, your tools and equipment, all your half-finished work."

Fust! Gutenberg's former partner, the man with

Opposite: As far as anyone knows, no portrait of Johann Gutenberg was painted in his lifetime. He certainly never had enough spare money to pay for his own portrait. This picture, based on a painting in the Gutenberg Museum in Mainz, shows him in the dress of a fifteenth-century German merchant and is possibly based on a sketch made by one of his colleagues.

Below: This view of a printshop shortly after Gutenberg's time would be familiar to many printers today. In the background, compositors are setting type by taking individual letters from a type case. In front, the printer's assistant inks the type surface with a leather pad while the printer checks the printed sheets.

whom the printer had shared the secrets of his invention!

"But what use is it to him?" he asked. "He knows nothing of printing. All he knows about is money."

"There is something else, master. Your foreman Peter Schoeffer is to join him. They are to set up a new printing works."

"A new printing works? With *my* equipment and even *my* foreman?"

"And Peter says there will be work with him for as many of your men who want it."

"And what about you, Heinrich, and you, Bechtolf? Will you join Fust and Schoeffer?"

The two men looked at the floor again. "We have to live, master," they muttered.

When they had gone, Gutenberg sat at his table and put his head in his hands. Everyone – even the men he had taught everything they knew about printing – had left him. He had nothing. It was the end of a dream.

A world without print

It is almost impossible to imagine a world in which printing – newspapers, magazines, books, maps, leaflets, posters – is not part of everyday life. Yet it was not until the middle of the fifteenth century that development in the printing field began. The printing of books using individual letters is only about five hundred and fifty years old.

But the fact that there was no printing in the western world until the fifteenth century does not mean that there were no books. Many of the world's great books were written before printing was invented. In English literature these included *Beowulf*, *The Anglo-Saxon Chronicle*, and Geoffrey Chaucer's *Canterbury Tales*. There were also Latin translations of the Bible and other religious books. But the only way of producing more than one copy of these books was by copying them out painstakingly, using a quill pen. In the Middle Ages, large numbers of people – mostly monks – worked as scribes, or book-copiers.

Royal courts and castles, as well as monasteries, housed collections of books, all copied out by hand

"The multiplication of books by writing with the pen is a slow process and peculiarly liable to inaccuracies, and the desire for a more satisfactory substitute must have often made itself felt through the ages among the literate."

Victor Scholderer, from "Johann Gutenberg".

on vellum made from stretched animal skin. Scribes would often relieve the boredom of their work by adding illustrations and decorations to the text, and this set a style which was copied by the early printers.

Boring

Hand-copying was a lengthy task. Someone who ordered a book would have to wait years for it. There was a shortage of scribes – not surprisingly, because it was demanding and poorly-paid work.

But time was not the only disadvantage of hand-copying. Bored or sleepy scribes might let their attention wander, or make mistakes through copying in poor light. Some scribes made their own "improvements" to the books they were copying. Others used their own system of abbreviations. The result was that many copies of books were "corrupt" – that is, they contained mistakes, or passages left out, or extra passages put in. When books were translated at the same time as they were being copied, from Latin into English for example, mistakes were even more likely to happen.

The copying of books by hand made the spread of new ideas very slow and laborious. Scientists might work out new theories and write a book about them: if they could not afford to have copies made, their ideas would live only between the covers of one book and might easily be lost when they died. The result was that people time and again "re-discovered" knowledge and worked to solve problems that had already been solved. After printing was invented in Europe, knowledge and ideas leapt ahead many times faster than they had before. Printing was one of the main reasons for the explosion of ideas in the fifteenth and sixteenth centuries known as the Renaissance.

Copying books by hand was a tedious and time-consuming task. This picture, dated about 1430, shows Jean Mielot, a French monk who was secretary to the Duke of Burgundy, at his copying desk. Thirty years later, printing from movable type had been invented and the need for this kind of work was disappearing.

The first printers

The true inventors of printing were the Chinese. By the ninth century – six centuries before any Europeans – they were carving complete pages of text on to wooden blocks and were taking copies

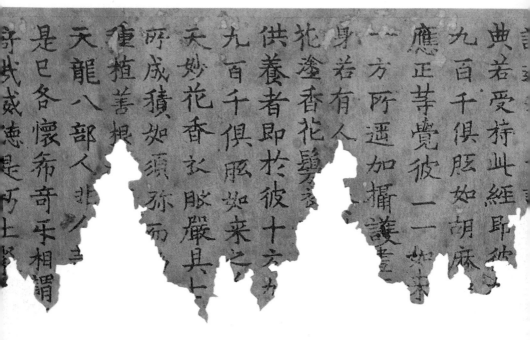

Carved wooden blocks, each carrying a character of the Chinese alphabet, were used in China over one thousand years ago. This example dates from 975. The Chinese had progressed some way in the development of printing, but the art was lost and had to be "rediscovered" by the western world.

from them. Later, they carved letters of the Chinese alphabet on to separate blocks that could be used again and again.

But the idea of printing did not spread beyond the Chinese empire, because there was very little communication between China and the rest of the world. In any case, the Chinese alphabet is very different from those of Middle Eastern and western civilizations so the Chinese method could not be adapted easily. But another product of Chinese inventiveness, paper, *had* spread to Europe by the eleventh century and was first made in Germany around 1390. It was well established by Gutenberg's time and made large scale printing projects a possibility.

The Chinese were making paper around AD 105. They beat linen rags into a pulp with water, and left the pulp to drain through a wire mesh. The matted threads dried into a sheet of paper. Small amounts of expensive writing paper are still made by this method today, though almost all paper is made by machine out of wood pulp.

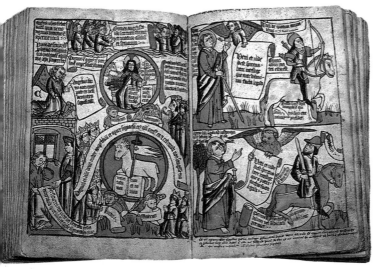

There were
libraries before
the invention of
movable type. The
books were either
hand-copied or
printed from
wooden blocks on
which both text
and illustrations
had been carved.
Above: Pope
Sixtus IV visits the
Papal Library in
Rome. Left:
Pages from a
block-book
showing part of
the Bible.

9

In the seventh century AD, Japanese courtiers were sent to China to learn more about Chinese art and technology. One of the skills they brought back was that of papermaking, at which the Japanese later became very proficient. This Japanese print shows the method, including the critical process of collecting beaten rags on a perforated screen.

Hand papermaking took time, but it was quicker than preparing vellum from animal skin which had to be cleaned, tanned and beaten. Paper was lighter and more regular in thickness, while being almost as strong and durable as vellum. And it was cheaper.

As knowledge of papermaking gradually spread westwards, other materials were experimented with. Many different types of plant could be used, but one of the most successful was flax, the plant from which linen is made. The use of paper spread quickly, and by 1450 it was taking the place of vellum except for legal and other important documents.

Supply and demand

Just before the Renaissance, there was a crisis in the world of books. There had been a huge increase in the number of churches and monasteries. Each needed its own copy of the Bible, together with prayer books and books of psalms. Increasing numbers of noble families, too, were demanding books to fill the libraries of their mansions and castles. In earlier times, a rich family might be judged by the amount of land it owned, or by the number of soldiers it could send to war. Now, the mood was changing. Rich people wanted to be thought of as cultured and learned, and aimed to fill their homes with works of art – and with books.

The scribes could not keep up with the demand. It must have occurred to many people to search for a way of producing books more quickly and cheaply. As they were experimenting on their own and kept no written records, nothing definite is known about them, but it is likely that in the Netherlands, Italy, and possibly in France people were, unknown to each other, working toward the invention of printing. There was a good reason for them to work in secret: there was no patent law to stop the copying of someone else's invention.

There are two main processes involved in printing. The first is setting the type – that is, making up separate letters into words, and words into lines – and arranging it in page form. The second is making copies by pressing paper against the type when it has been inked. The second process presented no problem, even in the fifteenth century. Presses for fruit – to press apples for cider-making, for example – were already widely used. They were operated by turning a screw which pressed two blocks of wood together. This idea could easily be adapted to printing. Books with pictures, and then later with captions beneath the pictures, were printed in Europe from solid carved wooden blocks. Even whole pages of text were reproduced in this way and many examples can still be found in museums today.

But this method was no use for printing large numbers of books. Carving enough blocks for a whole book – one block for each page – would have taken an army of skilled workers. The cost of their work would have made printed books as expensive – and almost as slow to produce – as books copied by hand.

Movable type

The key to printing lay in using movable type – separate pieces of wood or metal for each letter of the alphabet; capitals as well as lower case, each

"I was convinced that no wood-engraver would be capable of making wooden types in such a way that they would remain mathematically square."
Charles Enschede, a Dutch engraver who tried to imitate metal type in wood.

Incapit prologus sci ieronimi ar

fr bibliotecam de oibus diuineh

brosius michi tua munuscula

detulit simul 7 suauissimas litter

numeral, and each punctuation mark. These could then be put together to make the text for a few pages of a book. When these pages had been printed, the type could be taken apart and made up again for the next pages. Even for a single page of, say, the Bible, thousands of pieces of type would be needed. They would have to be precision-made so that they fitted together closely and in line.

Wood-carving was already a highly-skilled craft, but the degree of precision needed made it impossible to produce the small type necessary for the text of a book in this way. Besides, wood is easily damaged and worn, and does not stay in good condition for very long. What was needed was a breakthrough in technology.

Rival claims

The question of "who got there first" was once a matter of great debate among experts in the history of printing. According to some, a Dutchman,

Above: A hand-copied book represented months of work and was very valuable. Owners of books often chained them loosely to library shelves so that they could be opened and read, but not taken away. In churches, the Bible was often chained to the lectern.

Opposite: Before books were printed, no two copies of the same text were ever exactly alike. Sometimes, scribes would introduce corrections or "improvements" of their own. Extensive decorative work would also be added by the scribe.

In this portrait of Gutenberg, his fingers seem to be holding a stick into which type would be placed. The artist has neatly summed up what it was that made Gutenberg's invention distinctive – the selection of individual characters from an alphabet of type.

Laurens Coster of Haarlem, was the first to use movable type in 1423. Others claimed that an Italian, Pampilo Castaldi, led the way. It is known that a Czech living in Avignon in France, Procopius Waldfoghel, was working on "writing artificially" in 1444. But it is now generally agreed that the invention should be credited to Johann Gutenberg of Mainz.

After looking at all the claims and the evidence, experts have decided that, although others may have been working along the same lines, it was Gutenberg who first achieved the printing of a book using movable type. And the growth and spread of printing through Europe and to North America can be traced back clearly to Gutenberg's work in Mainz, in Germany, in the early 1450s.

Mystery man

Printing was probably the most important development in the history of Western civilization. For someone credited with such a world-shaking invention, Johann Gutenberg is a mysterious figure. For long periods of his life he disappeared from view, and nothing is known of what happened to him in those years. No one knows whether or where he went to school, whether or who he married, or exactly when or where he was born. The date of his death, February 3, 1468, is almost certain, but he was not thought important enough for his grave to be marked.

Even less would be known about him if it were not for a strange feature of his character: he spent much of his life involved in court cases. There was a dispute about his father's will, and another about money due to his mother. A woman named Anna took him to court because, she said, he had gone back on his promise to marry her. A shoemaker sued Gutenberg for calling him a liar and a cheat. Almost to the end of his life, Gutenberg was involved in cases against people who owed him, or had lent him, money.

It is mainly from the records of these cases that the story of his life can be pieced together. There is some guesswork in the scene at the beginning of this book, but the court case that resulted in Gutenberg's loss of his business was real enough. And it is a fact that, rather than face the pain of hearing the result, he sent Heinrich Keffer and Bechtolf von Hanau to hear it for him.

Little is known about Gutenberg's personality, but his frequent appearances in court suggest that he might have been a prickly character, quick to take offence. He was in financial trouble of one sort or another for most of his life. He seems to have been a poor businessman; if he ever hoped to make a fortune through his invention he failed, though printers all over Europe and beyond made handsome profits from it.

Comfortable beginnings

Gutenberg was born, probably in Mainz, around 1398. Mainz, on the banks of the River Rhine in Germany, was a busy trading town and the capital of one of the states that made up the Holy Roman Empire. Its leading citizen was the Archbishop of Mainz, whose rights included the minting of coinage for the state. This activity had attracted craftworkers in precious metals to the city, and Mainz had become famous for jewel accessories, metal-polishing, gold and silverwork.

Gutenberg's family was quite wealthy. Both his father, Friele, and his uncle were officials at the Archbishop's mint, and it was probably there that Johann learned the art of precision metalwork. Producing coinage demanded the careful and accurate casting and stamping of gold, an understanding of metals and temperature, and the use of casting chambers, dies and presses.

Because of his family connections, Johann did not have to serve as an apprentice. This meant that he was not tied to the mint when he had finished his training, and was free to leave whenever he wanted to. At the Archbishop's mint, he would have watched molten gold and silver being poured into casting chambers to make coins for the state, pressed, cooled and finally polished. It must have been there he had the first inkling of the idea that was to make his fame, though not his fortune.

tyes de octauis aduent' ⁊ de bã
maria. ad complectoriū ymn.
O venerande pōtif. cū cetis. ãt. Glam
mūdi. ꝑ. Sunt dimit OR. Ds q̃ bm
uel. Illumina qs domine. In conce
ptione beate mariē. ad vū aūt.

laude mr̄ ecia̅ nona festiuitas
gaudia lux micat. caligine
rosa de spine germie. ꝑ. Laud piu. ã.
Hec est illa stella maris ꝑ qñ fulg
lux solans annis festum celebremus
⁊ uniamen implorennus.ꝑ L aud do
omis qs. ã. O maria deuisus ortus
nautragantis mūdi port̄ placa no
bis qui te serie mr̄m ꝓ qñ elegit.
ꝑ. Lauda anima mea. ã. Acctio iam
suppliab; nr̄s fauendo jnb; magni
benignam ꝑorige vitamqꝫ mr̄am
dirige. ꝑ. L aud do. q̃ ben̄ ã. Audi virgo

glifica p̄ tiluum spes vnica dem dē
⁊ impiosa mr̄a dele maculosa ac
ceptans nr̄a cantica impetra pu
celica. ꝑ. Lauda ierusalem. Ca
gredietur virga de rad
desse ⁊ flos de radice eu
asendet. Deo gratias. ⁊ cordi
uris iubilo pangamus laudes d
Cuius nr̄s conceptio mūdū ꝑ
dit gaudio. v. Suscipe deuote ꝑ
ma xp̄e catenie. Cuius nr̄s. ymn.
sancta mundi dn̄a re
celi melita o stella mar
maria virgo mater detrica.
gr dulcis filia mestie iam virg
la florem latina nobilem ꝑ
deū ⁊ homin eni. Concepi
tu amia en columus sole̅
q̃ stirpe athletissima mūdo
sti genita. Per te sumus
gene simul eꝫ ac celigerie pac
pace nobili more in estimab
Sit trinitati glia sit dec
victoria in vnitate solidi ꝑ
secula amen. v. Egredietur
de radice jesse. Et flos de ra ã.
ans igneum. aue iubar ethec
nob pñs solemnitas da sit ꝑ
ditas tua vñꝫ conceptio sum
gratulatio alleluya. ꝑ. a ꝫ a
mplicatione fuox
deus miserator exa

Life in Mainz was not easy. There were continual struggles for power between the leading families, and between them and the Church. When one side gained control of the city, it would order its enemies to leave. The Gutenberg family were leading citizens, related by marriage to the mayor, and could not avoid getting involved in the city's politics. In 1411 Friele Gutenberg was forced to leave Mainz for a while, though his wife and children stayed there. In 1428, after Friele's death, Johann left to make a new home at Strasbourg, two hundred kilometres up the river Rhine. He made Strasbourg his home for approximately the next twenty years.

Opposite: A page from a fifteenth century hand-copied Bible. Decorations to the pages, usually added when the complete text had been finished, provided the scribe with welcome relief from the tedium of copying. They also gave added pleasure to the reader – and added value to the book itself.

Exile

It seems likely that he made his living in Strasbourg as a craftsman, and possibly a dealer, in accessories and precious metals. He may also have traded in other goods, for in 1439 he paid tax on nearly two thousand litres of wine. He was certainly not wealthy enough to have kept this amount of wine for his own use, so it may have been part of his business. Another possibility is that he was using the wine business as a cover for his real interest, experimenting with movable type.

Wine cellars would provide him with convenient premises in which he could work undisturbed, with no questions asked. The cities along the Rhine were central to the wine trade, the river providing a cheap means of transport. Dealing in wine was an ordinary business which would go almost unnoticed in a wine-trading city.

By this time Gutenberg had started on the experiments that were to lead to his first printed book some twenty-five years later. That book – the first printing known to have used Gutenberg's type – was so well produced, so nearly perfect, that it cannot have been his first effort. At this stage, he had solved so many of the technical problems that printing methods remained virtually unchanged for nearly four hundred years.

New inventions do not reach such perfection in

"He [Gutenberg] was a man with a ruling passion, and once he had found the channel that gave him at least the reward of achievement, he stayed in it, working out a principle of printing that was to survive unaltered into the nineteenth century."

Sean Jennett, from "Pioneers in Printing".

Although women were not allowed to benefit from university education, the wives and daughters of rich families took advantage of the libraries in convents and family houses.
Reading helped to widen the horizons of women whose lives were largely restricted to domestic duties.

one step. They involve years of trial and error, the discarding of ideas and starting again, apparent failure, endless perseverance. Gutenberg must also have had to fit in his experimental work with earning a living, so progress must have been slow. All this is what must have occupied Gutenberg during his "lost years" in Strasbourg in the 1430s and 1440s. There is no evidence. No trial runs of Gutenberg's printing have been found. But that is not surprising as it was a secret. No clues could be given to possible rivals.

Partnership

But there *is* evidence that *something* – something mysterious – was going on.

It is provided by a document drawn up in 1438.

This was a partnership agreement between Gutenberg and three Strasbourg men, Hans Riffe, Andres Heilmann and Andres Dritzehen. As so often happened with Gutenberg's affairs, there was a quarrel between him and his partners which resulted in a court case heard in 1439. It is from the reports of the case that it is possible to piece together some of what Gutenberg was doing in Strasbourg in the 1430s.

It seems that Gutenberg had invented a process and agreed to teach it to his three partners in return for a fee and loans of large sums of money. The partners promised not to pass on the secret, and if any of them died Gutenberg would buy out their share of the business. But what was the secret process? Naturally, it was not described in the agreement, but during the hearing it was mentioned that

This picture of St. Augustine, founder of Christianity in southern England, in his study was painted in the late fifteenth century, more than eight hundred years after St. Augustine's death. In fact, the study would not have been so well-furnished or spacious but it shows a fifteenth-century view of how a learned man would work.

some of the money had been used to buy lead and other metals, and a press. One of the witnesses said that he had lent Gutenberg some money "in connection with printing." This is the first time in Gutenberg's story that printing is linked with his name.

At Christmas 1438 one of the partners, Andres Dritzehen, died suddenly. It seems that in his house at the time was a tool, or instrument, which was a vital part of Gutenberg's secret process. It was said to have been made in four parts which could be screwed together. Separately, the four parts were like a puzzle and no one could have worked out their use. Put together, they revealed the secret. When Andres Dritzehen died, Gutenberg sent anxious messages to his house ordering that the mysterious piece of equipment should be taken apart. But it could not be found. Gutenberg also ordered something that they had made to be melted down. If this "something" was type, which seems likely, then Gutenberg must have been in a panic to have destroyed the fruits of several years' work.

The process of minting coins, which Gutenberg knew through his family and in which he may have trained, involved many of the techniques used to produce type. The impressions on the faces of coins were made by pressing hard metal dies on to "blanks" made of softer metal. In printing, the pieces of type were made in the same way.

The secret mirrors

Whatever the "something" was, this means of concealing its purpose was not the only undercover operation Gutenberg and his partners engaged in during these years. They seem to have set up yet another dummy business. A pilgrimage to the ancient city of Aachen, near the French border, was planned for 1439. The partners put it about that they had developed a new and secret way of making mirrors, and planned to sell these to the Aachen pilgrims.

This was an unlikely story. Aachen was about three hundred kilometres from Strasbourg – too far to make it worthwhile setting up a business for such a temporary and local trade. There was no reason why pilgrims in particular should need mirrors. There was no mention of the buying of materials to make mirrors. And whatever secret method Gutenberg and his partners had found, no revolutionary way of mirror-making emerged. What did it all mean?

Scholars have come up with one possible answer, though there is no way of proving it. There was a popular religious book which had been circulated in hand-copied form for about three hundred years. Its title was *The Mirror of Salvation*. This was just the sort of book that pilgrims might like to buy to read on their journey. Could it have been that Gutenberg's "secret process" was not for the making of mirrors, but for making printed copies of *The Mirror of Salvation?*

First steps

The agreement with Riffe and Heilmann came to an end in 1443. But it seems possible that Gutenberg had perfected movable type by that time and had started printing. The oldest example of printing from movable type is a scrap of paper with eleven printed lines on each side. The typeface is similar to one known to have been used by Gutenberg later. Experts have dated it to 1442. An almanac, or star calendar, for 1448, which would have been printed the year before, and a Latin grammar have

also been traced to Gutenberg, although nothing that he printed had his name on it.

Unlike most of the industries of that time, such as weaving and spinning, printing could not be carried on at home. So Gutenberg would have needed premises – large enough to hold the presses, stocks of new paper and printed sheets, with room to dry the printed sheets and collate or put in order the pages of books. He would have needed money to build his presses and make his type, to buy paper and ink, and to pay perhaps twenty workers – and none of this money would come back until the work was finished and the books sold. His workers would have to be trained in the ways of a new industry. The only way he could make the printing business pay was to make as much use as possible of his presses and type. Machinery and workers standing idle make no money.

It is possible that most of his work was in what is called "jobbing" printing – the printing of small items that are used and then thrown away. A jobbing printer today prints such things as tickets, letter-heads, leaflets and posters. There was no place for these things in fifteenth-century life, but there was a need for something similar called an "indulgence".

Paying for confession

A religious person who had committed a sin could be "forgiven" by paying a sum of money to the Church. In return, he or she would be given a piece of paper saying that the sinner had confessed, was sorry, and had been forgiven. The piece of paper was called an "indulgence". It also acted as a receipt for the money. Indulgences were sold in great numbers – they were one of the Church's main sources of money – by "pardoners" who kept some of the money themselves in return for their trouble.

It would have been convenient to have indulgences printed instead of painstakingly written out by hand. In the sixteenth century, it became the rule to have them printed, and so many were sold, with huge profits to the Church, that the scandal led to the separation of the Protestant and Roman Catholic churches at the Reformation. It is known that, later, Gutenberg printed indulgences in Mainz, and it may be that he was doing so as early as the 1440s in Strasbourg.

This information leads to yet another possibility. Early printers took the lettering of the scribes as their models, and sometimes it would have taken an expert to tell the difference between a hand-copied indulgence and a printed one. If, perhaps in league with a pardoner, Gutenberg was printing indulgences and passing them off as handwritten ones, he could have made a good profit. This might also explain the secrecy of the operation and the fact that only one fragment of Gutenberg's Strasbourg work has come to light. But if he made any money this way, it disappeared. Gutenberg was always short of money.

The cover of a hand-copied prayer book from the ninth century. Ivory carvings showing scenes from the life of Christ are inlaid into the wood. Makers of books regarded their work almost as an act of worship, especially in the monasteries, and were prepared to devote infinite time and effort into producing things of beauty.

Back in business

It is not known whether, after the partnership agreement ended in 1443, Gutenberg worked on alone in Strasbourg or whether he moved back to Mainz. He was certainly back in Mainz by 1448, when he borrowed a large sum of money from a banker there. (The money, like most of Gutenberg's debts, was never repaid.) But this was evidently not enough to carry Gutenberg's business forward, and he looked for someone else who would lend him more. His search led him to Johann Fust, a citizen of Mainz.

It is not certain what Fust's business was. Some historians of printing describe him as a goldsmith, others as a lawyer, others as a banker. He certainly had something that Gutenberg lacked – a head for business. Whatever his profession, Gutenberg must have convinced him that the plan for printing from movable type was far enough advanced to be likely to make money. Gutenberg's reputation for debt was well-known, since his debtors had so often taken him to court. Yet despite this, in 1450, Fust made Gutenberg a large loan of four hundred guilders. They agreed that if Gutenberg failed to repay the money plus interest, Fust would take over his equipment.

Two years later Fust lent Gutenberg another four hundred guilders, although none of the first loan, nor any of the interest on it, had been paid back. This time Fust protected his money by entering into a partnership which, as so often with Gutenberg, was later to end in a court case. But Gutenberg must have made enough progress for Fust to think it was worthwhile to go on investing. As it turned out, he was right.

The breakthrough

During the early 1450s, with Fust's money and his own hard work, Gutenberg perfected his method of casting type – and of casting enough to set about printing his chosen work, the Bible.

Others who had experimented with movable type had used wood. Wood-carving was already a well-developed craft and it was natural, since it is an easily-worked material, to turn to wood to solve the problem of producing type. But even large, angular type of the kind used by Gutenberg would have demanded extra special wood-carving skills, and the work involved in producing thousands of pieces of type would have occupied every carver in Europe for years. Wooden type was used widely until fairly recently, and is still used by a few traditional printers, in the very large sizes needed for posters. It has never been used for mass production of books. Apart from the work of producing it, even tiny inaccuracies would result in letters being out of line. The noticeable feature of all Gutenberg's work is how well-aligned the letters are. As an experiment, a number of wood-carvers in the past have tried to produce small type precise enough for book work, but none have succeeded.

Adaptation

In the fifteenth century, coins were made by pouring molten metal into shapes and letting it set into coins called blanks. These were then re-heated, and a punch with the coin's design, called the die, was pressed into each blank. Great pressure was needed to make a good, clear impression, and mints used huge screw presses which were operated by two men on each arm of the press.

It was natural that Gutenberg, having spent years watching this process in action, should think of adapting it to produce type in a similar way. But in adapting the idea from making coins to producing print Gutenberg faced a number of problems.

Only a few different coins are needed to make up a currency. Japan, for example, manages with six. To cover the upper and lower case alphabet, numerals and punctuation marks, Gutenberg needed to cast type from over sixty different shapes. All must be as accurate as those for coins, and they must also fit precisely with any of the others. Then there was the question of which metals to use. Coins were normally made of gold or silver, with small additions of other metals to make them harder and longer-lasting: Gutenberg needed a metal that was

"A room without books is as a body without a soul."
Lord Avebury, 1834-1913.

Opposite: The Gutenberg Museum at Mainz in Germany includes a faithful reproduction of Gutenberg's printshop as it would have been in the 1450s. This is a replica of Gutenberg's original printing press.

cheap, and which melted easily. And he could not afford to buy or fuel the huge furnaces which were used at the mint.

He must have made many attempts before he hit on the solutions to these problems, especially on what metals to use, but the method he eventually worked out remained in use for over five hundred years – and this is why Gutenberg is acclaimed as the inventor of movable type. Typefounding by machine, invented in the nineteenth century, used just the same principle, and it is only in the past forty years that photographic typesetting has been developed.

Casting type

He probably began with the brass punches that bookbinders used. Each carried a letter of the alphabet reversed from left to right, and was used to stamp the title of a hand-copied book on its surface. If a similar punch were used on a bar of a softer metal, such as brass, an impression could be indented in the same way. And if the brass was then used as a cast for a still softer metal such as lead, copies of the original die could be produced. But the process had to be simple and fast.

Many thousands of characters – letters, punctuation marks, and blank pieces of type for the spaces – would be needed for a few pages of a book. Each full page of text in this book, for example, uses over 1,800 characters. It has been estimated that two pages of Gutenberg's Bible would have needed about six thousand pieces of type. Also, the depth of each piece of type had to be exactly the same, or some letters would print heavily while others would make only a faint mark. The evenness of the print in Gutenberg's work shows how precisely his type must have been cast.

First then, Gutenberg – or a craftsman specially hired for the job – would have cut a punch for each character by hand, taking a "proof" or impression from it until it was perfect. It would be checked

"Johann Gutenberg invented printing before the middle of the fifteenth century. Typography is a more correct term, for what he did was to construct the apparatus for making movable metal letters or type and for using these to produce many copies, all alike, of a book."
George Parker Winship, from "Gutenberg To Plantin".

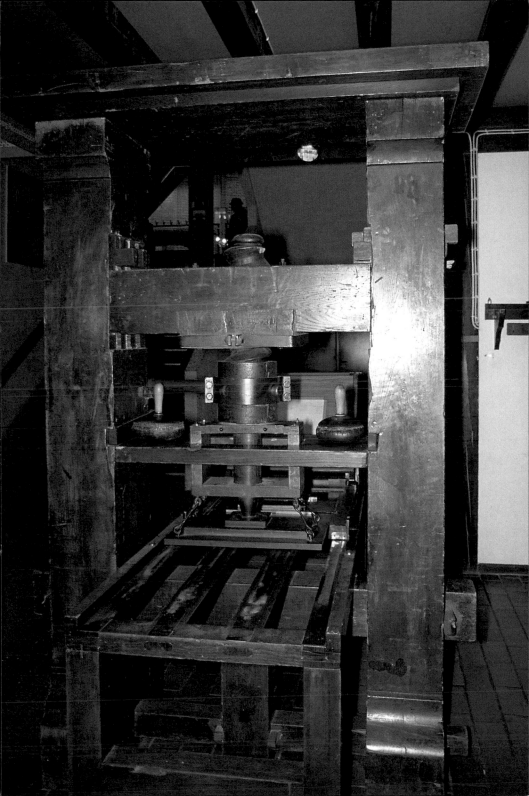

and improved if necessary with the use of a file or engraving tool. This was important, because the die for the letter *a* for example, would be the model for all the letters *a* in many books. When the craftsman was satisfied, the punch would be driven into a piece of brass, leaving an indented impression called the matrix. The matrix, then, was the receptacle for the molten metal which formed the letter part of the type.

In letterpress printing, each piece of type must be cut precisely so that it fits tightly to the next. Blank pieces of wood or metal are used to fill up any spaces. When the type has been set, it is "locked up" in a forme , which prevents it from moving during printing. This illustration comes from an eighteenth-century French encyclopaedia.

The next problem was to make a shape accurate enough to make each piece of type exactly the same height. It seems that Gutenberg may have used just one single shape for the whole of a set, or fount, of type, changing the matrix as necessary. This would make sure they were all the same height. But it would have been necessary to be able to alter the *width* of that shape, to cope with the different widths of letters of the alphabet, for example *m* and *i*. He overcame this by making two L-shaped pieces which slid into each other and so adjusted the space between them. In this way, it could be used for any of the letters of the alphabet, or for punctuation marks. It was probably an early version of this that disappeared at Andres Dritzehen's house and caused Gutenberg so much anxiety in 1438.

The matrix, to form the letter face, was placed in the bottom of this L-shaped casting chamber and molten lead poured in. When the lead was set, the metal could be tapped out as a single piece of cast type. Many copies of that letter were produced before the matrix was replaced with another.

Preparation

The finished pieces of type were stored in cases, and pictures of early printing workshops show cases similar to those familiar to all printers until fairly recently. The compositor, or typesetter, then picked out the letters needed and put them temporarily into a holder called a "stick" with blank pieces of type to make the spaces between words. The type was then transferred from the stick and placed on a tray, or galley. The spacing between the lines was inserted at this stage. When a whole page had been made on the galley it was placed into a steel or iron frame. The page of type was then made secure in this frame ready for printing – wedges were hammered in at the edges to keep the type firmly in place. Once it was secure it was called a "forme" and was ready to be put in the press.

Going to press

The first printing presses were made of wood. The forme was placed on the base of the press, which was called the "bed". Printers still talk of "putting a paper to bed", meaning to see it on to the press. The type was inked with a leather pad. The printer laid a sheet of paper carefully over the type, and brought down a second block of wood by means of a large screw which had two long arms fitted to it, with a man for each arm as this was heavy work. Once printed, the paper was hung up to dry.

Each individual printing could not be hurried, and even the most careful worker must have produced many copies spoilt by smudges. Yet the quality of Gutenberg's Bible is high; a great deal of trial and error would have gone into achieving such high standards. It must have been the greatest disappointment of Gutenberg's life that, after years of experiment and struggle, he had his triumph snatched away from him.

For about three hundred years after Gutenberg, the wooden screw press was the only kind in use. The speed of printing was restricted by the time taken to operate the screw downwards to print and upwards to release the paper. Great skill was needed to avoid smudges and achieve just the right amount of pressure between type and paper. Printing with a screw press also involved a good deal of physical stamina, and printers were usually, as here, burly, powerful men.

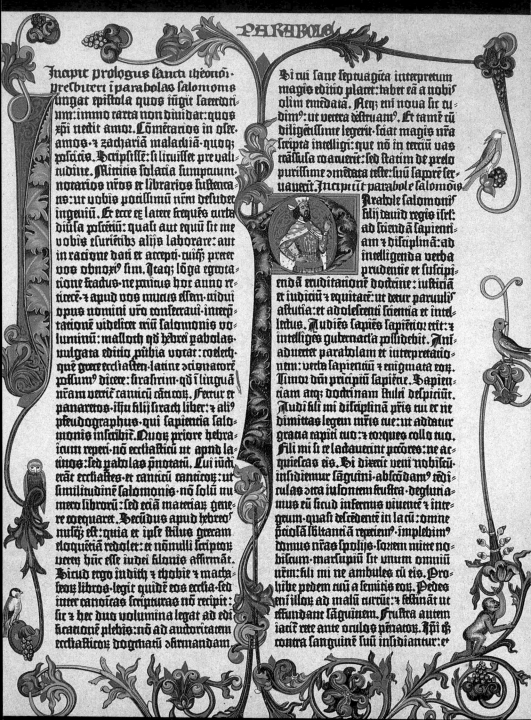

Incipit prologus sancti iheronimi presbiteri in parabolas salomonis.

ungat epistola quos iungit sacerdotium: immo carta non diuidat: quos xpi nectit amor. Comentarios in osee. amos. z zachariam malachiam quoq; poscitis. Scripsissem: si licuisset pre valitudine. Mittitis solacia sumptuum. notarios nostros et librarios sustentandis: ut vobis potissimum nrm desudet ingeniu. Et ecce ex latere frequens turba diuersa poscentium: quasi aut equum sit me vobis esurientibus aliis laborare: aut in racione dati et accepti. cuiuss preter vos obnoxius sim. Itaq; longa egrotatione fractus: ne penitus hoc anno reticerem: z apud vos mutus essem: huic opus nomini vro consecraui. interpretatione videlicet triu salomonis voluminu: masloth qd hebrei pabolas vulgata editio phibia vocat: coeleth. que grece ecclesiasten. latine cocionatore possum9 dicere: sirasim. qd i linguam nram vertit canticu canticoru. Fertur et panaretos. ihsu filij sirach liber: z aliUS pseudographus. qui sapientia salomonis inscribit. Quorum priore hebraicum reperi. non ecclesiasticum ut apud latinos: sed pabolas pnotatu. Cui iucti erat ecclesiastes. et canticu canticoru: ut similitudine salomonis. non solu numero librorum: sed etiam materiarum genere coequaret. Secundus apud hebreos nusq; est: quia et ipse stilus grecam eloquentiam redolet: et nonnulli scriptoru veteru hunc esse iudei filonis affirmat. Sicut ergo iudith z thobie z machabeoru libros. legit quidem eos ecclesia. sed inter canonicas scripturas non recipit: sic z hec duo volumina legat ad edificatione plebis: no ad auctoritatem ecclesiasticoru dogmatu cofirmandam.

Si cui sane septuaginta interpretum magis editio placet: habet eam a nobis olim emedata. Neq; enim noua sic cudimus9: ut vetera destruamus9. Et tame cu diligentissime legerit: sciat magis nra scripta intelligi: que non in tertium vas trasfusa coacuerit: sed statim de prelo purissime comedata teste: suu saporem seruauerit. Incipiut parabole salomonis.

Parabole salomonis filij dauid regis isrl: ad sciendam sapientiam z disciplinam: ad intelligenda verba prudentie et suscipienda eruditione doctrine: iusticia et iudicium z equitate: ut detur paruulis astucia: et adolescenti scientia et intellectus. Audies sapies sapientior erit: z intelliges gubernacla possidebit. Animaduertet parabolam et interpretatione: verba sapientiu z enigmata eoru. Timor dni principiu sapientie. Sapientiam atq; doctrinam stulti despiciut. Audi fili mi disciplinam patris tui et ne dimittas legem matris tue: ut addatur gracia capiti tuo: z torques collo tuo. Fili mi si te lactauerint peccatores: ne acquiescas eis. Si dixerint veni nobiscum: insidiemur sanguini: abscodamus9 tendiculas contra insontem frustra. degluciamus eu sicud infernus viuente z integrum: quasi descendente in lacu: omne preciosam substantiam reperiemus9. implebim9 domus nras spolijs. sortem mitte nobiscum. marsupiu sit unum omniu nrm: fili mi ne ambules cu eis. Prohibe pedem tuu a semitis eoru. Pedes enim illoru ad malu curruc: z festinat ut effundant sanguinem. Frustra autem iacit rete ante oculos pennatoru. Ipsi qz contra sanguine suu insidiantur: et

With his large loans from Fust, Gutenberg set about the printing of the Bible. He may have begun as early as 1450. It is thought by historians of printing that the work was certainly under way by 1452. Even with today's high-speed typesetting and presses printing thousands of pages per hour on reels of paper, this would be a mammoth undertaking. With each letter set by hand, and each sheet laboriously placed in the press, printed, taken out, dried and then printed on the reverse side, it hardly seems possible that anyone would have the courage to start. But once started there was no going back, because no money would come in until the job was completed and the Bibles sold.

The work dragged on. Johann Fust had to provide more money. It is said in an account written in 1474 that Gutenberg was printing three hundred sheets a day, using six presses. The Bible consists of 641 sheets, and it is thought that about three hundred copies were produced. This means that printing alone – after the type had been cast – would have taken at least two years. In fact, it seems to have taken a good deal longer, partly because it was decided, after some sheets had been printed, to increase the number of copies, so that some pages had to be set up in type a second time.

It may have been over this that Gutenberg and Fust fell out because in 1455 Fust took Gutenberg to court for the return of his money. This was the case to which Gutenberg sent his workmen. The money had been spent and could not be returned. Fust took over the press, the type and the completed Bibles – the entire business – in settlement of the debt.

The Gutenberg Bible

What had been produced was what is sometimes known as the "forty-two-line Bible" because almost all its pages contain forty-two lines in two columns, though some are a line or two shorter. There were 1,282 pages, bound in two volumes though probably the binding was done elsewhere and later. It is known that at least some copies of the Bible were sold as separate sheets, for the buyer to bind.

Opposite: A page from the "forty-two line Bible", Gutenberg's first printed book. For the design of his type, Gutenberg took as his model the lettering used by scribes. This was so successful that some people accused his partner, Fust, of trying to pass off printed Bibles as hand-copied ones to obtain a higher price.

Of the three hundred or so copies of the forty-two-line Bible that were printed, about forty still exist in museums and libraries in various parts of the world, including the New York Public Library, the British Library in London, and the Gutenberg Museum in Mainz.

The copies are not all exactly the same. In some, large initial capital letters at the start of new chapters were hand-painted, and in others type was used. Experts have reckoned that the Bible was printed in ten sections, which means that Gutenberg must have had enough type to set up about 130 pages at a time. If this is right, he would have used nearly four hundred thousand pieces of type, representing a huge investment of time and metal. It is clear that he had discovered a quick and easy way of making type, and this was his particular contribution to the history of printing.

Court

The period that led up to the dispute between Gutenberg and Fust is the only part of Gutenberg's life which is known about in any detail. A written account of Fust's accusations against Gutenberg has survived and is in the library of Gottingen University in Germany. Fust said that he had originally agreed to lend Gutenberg a sum of money at six per cent interest. Later, he doubled the amount, but complained that Gutenberg had paid no interest on either loan and was demanding the return of both loans and the unpaid interest.

Gutenberg had a different story but the most likely explanation of Gutenberg's careless way with money is that he was so obsessed with his ideas that he would take any risk to further them.

The amount at stake, including the interest claimed by Fust, was just over two thousand guilders. In the fifteenth century, two thousand guilders would have bought a herd of about 250 fat cattle. In other words, the case involved very large amounts of money in today's terms.

The outcome was that Gutenberg was ordered to repay Fust's first loan, with interest. Of course, he had spent the money, and so had to hand over his type, his presses, and all the work in hand. This included the forty-two-line Bible, which was nearly completed, and so Gutenberg never saw a penny profit from its sale. All he had to show for years of work was financial ruin.

After the case

Students of the history of printing take sides in the dispute between Gutenberg and Fust. It's natural to sympathize with Gutenberg, whose great work was taken over by someone else, but he had a bad record as a debtor. He seems to have borrowed money freely without any idea of whether he could

A letter from the Latin Psalter which was printed by Fust and Schoeffer in 1457. It was produced from metal blocks and printed at the same time as the text. Being able to print highly decorative letters such as this made scribes even more redundant.

A typical German court scene in the fifteenth century. Then, as now, courts dealt with business disputes as well as crime. It was a scene such as this that Gutenberg tried to avoid in November 1455 – but it was also one that he was familiar with throughout his life.

pay it back, and perhaps with no intention of ever doing so. The fact that, when the court case came up, Gutenberg sent Heinrich Keffer and Bechtolf von Hanau to report back to him suggests that he knew that he would lose the case.

But what about Johann Fust? The rate of interest he demanded from Gutenberg, six per cent, was high for the time. He claimed that this was because he had had to borrow the money from someone else so that there were two lots of interest to be paid. But it might be thought unfair of Fust to take over Gutenberg's business, and even his workforce, without offering Gutenberg himself a job – but Fust may have found Gutenberg difficult to work with and had had no return at all on his money.

Whatever the rights and wrongs of the court case, in his mid-fifties Gutenberg was left without work and, as it must have seemed to him, the invention to which he had given twenty years of his life in the hands of someone else. But fortunately, he was not without friends. Dr. Konrad Homery of Mainz lent him a press and type, which he kept for the rest of his life. Nothing is known for certain of anything that was printed on this press, and Gutenberg's last years passed in the shadows that clouded many periods of his life. All that is known is that he was given a pension, as a distinguished citizen of Mainz, in 1465 and that he died about three years later.

"Inventor"

Gutenberg never put his name on anything that he printed, which is one reason why there has been so much argument about him. He *may* have produced, as well as the forty-two-line Bible, a thirty-six-line Bible, a number of other religious books, some Latin grammars, many indulgences and other disposable material. But it is impossible to be certain. Some of these items that survive seem to have been printed with the type believed to have been used by Gutenberg, but this is not proof that he actually printed them. His type passed to Fust after the court case of 1455. In any case, the work and cost of producing a set of type was so immense that it would have been passed from one owner to another until it was worn out.

Perhaps it is surprising, in view of how little is known about Gutenberg, that he is now accepted as the inventor of printing or, more exactly, the inventor of printing from movable type. But most historians who have examined all the evidence, of which there is not very much, now agree that his claim is correct.

Gutenberg was first credited as "the inventor of printing" in a book published in Cologne in 1499, though claims for others were already being made in France, Holland and Italy. But even if he was not the very first printer to use movable type, it was his system and his equipment that led to the development of printing in Europe. Many of the printers who set up presses in other cities and other countries had been trained by Gutenberg in Mainz.

Certainties

After the 1455 court case, Johann Fust found himself the owner of a printing business, all the equipment needed to run it, and a stock of Bibles. He may have taken charge of the sale of the Bibles, but he had no practical experience of printing. This explains why he took care to offer Peter Schoeffer, Gutenberg's foreman, a job, and also gave work to a number of Gutenberg's other workers.

Schoeffer was a fine craftsman who went on printing until his death round about 1500. Here, the history of printing starts to include some certainties, for Fust and Schoeffer put their names on at least some work and were the first printers to do so.

The forty-two-line Bible evidently sold well, and probably provided the money for the printing of Fust and Schoeffer's own first book. This was a book of Psalms. It came out in 1457, and was the first book to carry both the date of publication and the name of the printers. It was reprinted again and again, using the same type, until 1516. Fust

"The types of the fifteenth century differed in no essential particular from those of the nineteenth. Ruder and rougher, and less durable they might be, but in substance and form, and in the mechanical principles of their manufacture, they claim kinship with the newest types of our most modern foundry."

Talbot Baines Reed, typefounder.

and Schoeffer were the first printers to adopt the practice, which later became standard, of storing the formes of type for future editions to save the expense of resetting.

During their partnership, which lasted until Fust's death in 1466, he and Schoeffer printed 115 books, including a forty-eight-line Bible. Comparing this rate of production, about twelve books a year, with Gutenberg's suggests that Gutenberg must either have been very slow or interrupted by technical or financial problems, and perhaps this was the cause of his split with Fust.

After Fust's death, Schoeffer continued the printing business and built it up until it covered virtually the whole of western Europe and included publishing and bookselling as well. But by that time, printing had escaped from Mainz and spread throughout Germany and beyond.

The age of print

The speed with which printing spread can be compared with that of the computer in the last half of the twentieth century, and it had just as dramatic an effect on the history of the time. Suddenly, people wondered how they had managed without it. It also, like the spread of the computer, had some side-effects. The computer put an end to the drudgery of clerical work for many people – but it put many of them out of a job. So did printing. The victims were the scribes, who took a year to do what a printing press could do in a few days. Some still found work decorating, or "illuminating" the printed pages, but soon this too could be done by the printer; Schoeffer himself was a pioneer printer of lavishly decorated books.

The spread of printing was helped by two events, one local to Mainz and the other more far-reaching.

In 1459, the Archbishop of Mainz died, and two rivals claimed the right to take his place. They declared war on each other, and the citizens of Mainz backed the loser. The winner took his revenge: the new Archbishop ordered all the men young and fit enough to fight, to leave the city.

This included a number of Fust and Schoeffer's printers. Gutenberg, who was still alive, was probably excused because of his age. But the younger printers hastily made their escape, moving along the rivers Rhine and Main which meet at Mainz. They set up new printing works at Bamberg, Strasbourg and Cologne. This set off a chain reaction which spread the craft of print throughout Europe and beyond. Monasteries set up printing works which gave work to the scribes whose hand-copying services were no longer needed. Presses were attached to places of learning such as universities and other pressworks were profitable businesses.

The speed with which the art of printing spread is astonishing. It seems as if Gutenberg's invention released a pent-up demand for books which could not be satisfied. In Italy, the first press was started, by two Germans, in Rome in 1464. In 1469 another

This woodcut showing a printshop was made in 1499, and shows Death seizing and carrying off the printers. What was in the artist's mind? Perhaps he was a scribe put out of work by the invention of printing, and imagining his revenge. Perhaps he was suggesting that printers were prone to illness – or even that by spreading knowledge printing was Death's enemy.

Above: Printers acquired the habit of "signing" their work by using a colophon which identified a book as printed by them. This was William Caxton's.

Below: The Vulgate was the first complete translation of the Bible into Latin. Made by St. Jerome in the fourth century AD, it became the standard version used in the Roman Catholic Church. This is the title page of a copy printed in 1528 in Venice.

German printer, John of Speier, set up his press in Venice, and within ten years Venice was the world capital of printing and publishing. There was a plentiful supply of paper, made in works supplied with water from the streams of northern Italy, and as the major seaport of southern Europe Venice was also a good distribution point. Meanwhile, in 1470 the first press in France started work, followed in 1471 by the Netherlands, in 1472 by Switzerland, in 1475 by Spain and in 1476 by England.

Reading for pleasure

England's printer – and the first printer in English – was William Caxton. He was a wealthy man who came to take an interest in printing through his love of literature. He printed about one hundred books before his death in 1491. Most of his output was books that would be read with pleasure and therefore sell well. Through Caxton and other printers like him, books began to be seen as a means of entertainment. Reading became something which everyone, especially women (who at that time had no part to play in religion or politics), could enjoy. Soon, reading became one of the "accomplishments" which well-brought-up young women of noble families prided themselves on, and reading aloud to the family and guests became a popular way of filling in long winter evenings. Books had come out of the scholar's study and into the home.

Fear

But it was not long before some people began to see dangers in the spread of printed books. One of printing's first enemies was the Roman Catholic Church. Until the fifteenth century, learning had been controlled by the Church. There were few schools, but the Church owned them and it ran the universities. Church services were sung in Latin, so that only educated people could translate them. The Bible was in Latin, and ordinary folk had to trust the priest's word when he told them what was in it. In these various ways, the Church was able to control what people believed, thought and how they lived their lives.

One of the first results of the invention of printing was that translations of the Bible began to appear in large numbers. The first German translation was printed in Strasbourg in about 1466, and was soon followed by French, Spanish and Dutch translations. For the first time, the Bible could be studied without the guidance of priests, and people who did so began to be critical of the Church. They noticed, for example, that in its early days Christianity had managed very well without popes and archbishops and all the other costly features of the fifteenth century Church. The early Christians had worshipped in simple buildings, not in richly-decorated cathedrals. There was nothing in the Bible about obtaining forgiveness for sins by buying indulgences. Altogether, the picture of Christianity in the New Testament was very different from what the Church had led people to believe.

"I have practised and learned at my great charge and dispense to ordain this said book in print, after the manner and form as ye may here see, and is not written with pen and ink as other books be, to the end that every person might have them at once. For all the books of this story were begun in one day and also finished in one day...."

William Caxton, in the Epilogue to the first printed edition of his "History of Troy".

William Caxton presents a copy of a new book to Edward IV of England.

39

Critics of the Church – often writing anonymously to avoid trouble – made full use of the printing press. The ideas they put forward in books and pamphlets played an important part in the Reformation – the breakaway movement which led to the foundation of the Protestant churches.

Banned

The Roman Catholic Church hit back. In 1546 it forbade the printing of anonymous books about religion unless they had been approved by the Church, and published a list of other forbidden books. Printing or publishing a forbidden book was heresy – preaching against the Church – and punishable by death. Books that were thought likely to encourage the spread of new religious ideas or make people question the teachings of the Church were banned.

Unlike Roman Catholic services, Protestant services involved everyone. The new Protestant churches in Europe needed supplies of the Bible, prayer books and hymn books in their national languages, and many Protestants went into the printing trade. Protestant printers who had been driven out of Britain were among the passengers on the *Mayflower* which carried the Pilgrim Fathers to North America in 1620.

The Pilgrim Fathers had a great respect for education, and as soon as they had settled in their new homes they began to build schools and colleges. Education needs books, and in 1638, a press was set up in Cambridge, Massachusetts, and was very quickly producing the first books to be printed in North America. They included books of psalms, school textbooks, and the Bible. The Cambridge press even printed a translation of the Bible into the language of the Algonquin native people of America.

But the Protestants of North America were no less frightened of the printed word than the Catholics of Europe. From the start, religious books had to be approved, and this law was later extended to cover all "books, pamphlets and other matter."

Opposite: One way of stopping the spread of books not approved of by the Church was to burn them. But although fire could destroy the printed word, it could not destroy ideas.

Below: A detail from a model of an early Italian printshop. The two printers in the foreground are proof-reading – checking the printed pages for mistakes. The other workman inks a forme of type ready for the press.

Printing and publishing did not become free of control until 1730.

The Pilgrim Fathers were not the first to take printing across the Atlantic. A century earlier, Roman Catholic priests from Spain had taken a press to Mexico, which was then a Spanish colony. From 1539, this press began to print religious books. Later, following the missionaries of the Roman Catholic Church, a press was set up in Peru. In Central and South America, printing was used not to attack the Church, but to spread its beliefs.

Printing the news

When, in 1588, the Spanish Armada threatened to invade England, the news that the Spanish fleet had been sighted was sent across the country by beacon fires lit on hilltops. This was unusual. News usually passed by word of mouth, or by letters between educated people who could read and write. Many printers tried to meet the demand for printed news, but it could be dangerous. A London man named William Prynne, who wrote a number of attacks on Charles I of England, was sentenced in 1634 to be fined five thousand pounds, have his ears cut off, spend a year in the Tower of London and have his university degree taken away. In the eighteenth century a Cologne newspaper printer who had criticized the government was almost killed by a thug paid to beat him up, and a Berlin printer was imprisoned and finally exiled for printing criticism of the government. In North America the first newspaper, published in Boston, Massachusetts in 1690, was banned after one issue, though the printer and publisher were not punished.

During the seventeenth century, some governments began to use printing to give information and orders to the people. Other governments saw dangers in the free circulation of news – and, even more, of opinions. Taxes on copies of newspapers, and on the advertisements which helped pay for them, were introduced.

There were other ways of controlling what newspapers printed. Writers were sometimes paid by the

Opposite: All early printing was slow, but the slowest process of all was setting the type. It demanded a large workforce of skilled and literate compositors. In the fifteenth and sixteenth centuries, the ability to read was not common, so compositors were an élite. They and the printers soon formed themselves into guilds to protect their craft and negotiate pay.

As printing spread, governments became alarmed at books and newspapers attacking them. There were many calls for the right of printers to print what they liked. Here, at the time of the French Revolution in 1789, campaigners in Paris are demanding freedom of the press.

government not to criticize it. *The Times* of London, which started in 1785 under the title of *The Daily Universal Register*, was paid by the Prime Minister of the day, William Pitt, not to attack him.

Chapbooks and broadsides

Until about one hundred years ago, newspapers were produced mainly for educated men interested in politics. The pages were made up of long columns of smudgy print reporting speeches and political meetings. There were no pictures. Such papers were of no interest to people who had had little, if any, education. Until this century, no women – except in New Zealand and parts of Australia – could vote in elections, so few had any interest in politics.

Books, too, were for educated people. They were

also too expensive for poor people to buy, and there were no public libraries until half-way through the nineteenth century. But these people were not without something to read. The advent of printing meant that *anyone* who could read suddenly had access to all kinds of written information – great discoveries, different cultures, tales and facts. Printers began to run off little booklets of a few pages, with paper covers and woodcut pictures. These were called chapbooks, and they were sold by chapmen or pedlars who went from village to village with such things as cheap toys, needles and thread and homely medicines. A chapbook would contain one or two folk tales or Bible stories, with perhaps a nursery rhyme or two. Chapbooks were intended for all the family to read. Often children, who were more likely to have been to school, read the stories to the others.

Broadsides were another popular form of cheap printing. They were crudely-printed song-sheets, containing only the words of songs but often suggesting a tune to which they could be sung. Broadsides were also sold by salesmen, at fairs and markets, from about 1650 onwards.

Some broadsides re-told old stories in verse, but others were about recent events in the news and so were, in a way, the "newspapers" of the people. The subjects of the broadsides were much the same as would appear on the front page of a popular newspaper today – crime and punishment, disasters, national occasions such as a coronation, and war. A big event like a battle would be quickly written up in verse, printed, and rushed out on to the streets. Broadsides on themes like this sold in thousands. The words of some of them are still sung today as folksongs, having been learnt by heart and passed by word of mouth down the generations.

Guilds

Although, by about 1800, printing was a major industry in many cities throughout Europe and North America, its technology had not changed since Gutenberg's time over three hundred years before. Printers had concentrated on the art, not

> *"If a book is worth reading, it is worth buying."*
> John Ruskin, art critic.

As government controls were relaxed in the nineteenth century, this led to a great explosion of printing. As books became cheaper, they reached an increasingly wide readership. Women, whose educational opportunities were still narrower than those of men, took to reading with great enthusiasm.

The *"Illustrated London News"* was a popular British weekly magazine in the nineteenth century, famous for its large engravings of events in the news. This picture from it shows a newspaper being printed on a ten-feeder rotary press in 1860.

the technology, of their trade. Many craftsmen such as William Caslon, Jean Claude Fournier, John Baskerville and, in North America, Benjamin Franklin designed typefaces which were good to look at and produced beautiful books. Typefaces based on their designs are still used today. But the Gutenberg method of printing remained in use largely because printers had taken care to protect their trade by forming "guilds". In some ways the guilds were similar to modern trade unions. For example, they negotiated rates of pay and hours of work and controlled the training of apprentices and the setting up of new printing businesses. In some countries they co-operated with the government in restricting the number of presses allowed to operate and the number of foundries allowed to cast type.

The guilds had little interest in improving methods of printing, because the traditional methods helped to make printing scarce and keep prices up. The result was that printing as a whole

was backward-looking. In the eighteenth and nineteenth centuries, printers were quite happy to go on using the methods their fathers had used; satisfaction with the old ways of doing things discouraged the development of new methods. This attitude continued, especially among newspaper printers, until very recently. Printers fought the introduction of new presses which allowed the high-speed printing of pictures in newspapers, and of computerized machines which speeded up typesetting. They had privileged, highly paid jobs that they wanted to protect. It is no accident that when improvements came they were developed mainly by people from outside the printing trade.

The first breakthrough came with the replacement of the screw on the press by a lever which pressed the block of wood down on to the paper. This was a much quicker operation, because while the screw had to be laboriously raised after each impression, the lever could merely be released so that the wood sprang upwards. The first lever press was built by Earl Stanhope, a British politician and scientist whose other inventions included a device for tuning musical instruments and a calculating machine. His was the first press to be made entirely of iron instead of wood. Lever presses began to be used about 1800. Some of these are still used by printers who concentrate on fine hand-printing, and also by wood-engravers.

Although the lever press was a great improvement, its output was still limited by the speed with which the paper could be placed in position, the lever operated, and the paper removed. But something new was just around the corner.

The Koenig press

Frederick Koenig, the next important name in the history of printing, was born in Leipzig in Germany in 1774. In some ways he was like Gutenberg. He too had an obsession with printing. With Koenig, it was an obsession with finding a way of printing more quickly and with less work. Like Gutenberg, he had no money and depended on finding backers for his ideas.

"The printer was ordinarily also a retailer, having a bookstore in front of his house or shop. There he sold the works he printed, as well as others which he secured by exchanging his productions for those from the presses of rival printers living in the same or nearby towns."
George Parker Winship, from "Gutenberg To Plantin".

Koenig had been apprenticed as a printer, but gave up his training to study at the University of Leipzig. After that he seems to have disappeared from view, a young man with no particular interest in engineering or mechanics, until he turned up at the age of about thirty in Suhl, 150 kilometres from Leipzig, running an engineering workshop. By this time he had made a printing press that worked by a system of pulleys. His unsuccessful search for orders for this machine led him to various parts of Germany, to Russia and eventually to London. There, he had a stroke of good luck. He was introduced to John Walter II, the owner and editor of *The Times* newspaper. The year was 1812.

The Times had been started, as *The Daily Universal Register,* almost by accident. Its founder John Walter – the father of John Walter II – had made a fortune as a coal merchant and lost it as a

From western Europe, printing spread rapidly to other countries and cultures. As in Europe, it was seen as a valuable means of spreading religious thought. An important effect of printing was that it enabled the texts of holy books such as the Bible and the Koran to be "fixed", free from errors introduced by scribes.

dealer in insurance. He then became interested in the technology of printing, and in particular in an idea for faster typesetting by using "logotypes" – single pieces of type made up of the most commonly-used words and parts of words. He started *The Daily Universal Register* in order to demonstrate the system. Logotypes came to nothing, but the paper itself prospered, helped partly by the war with France which broke out in 1793, which increased people's appetite for news.

But by 1812 *The Times* was in trouble. John Walter II was unable to print enough copies to satisfy the demand. The only way to increase the output was to buy more presses and have the same type set many times over – a costly business which also meant delays in getting the latest news on to the streets. Newspapers depend on the speed of their operation. If they are late coming out, then they might as well not come out at all. When Koenig demonstrated his latest machine, which could print over one thousand sheets an hour, John Walter II gave him an order for two presses then and there.

Steam

Koenig's press was a steam printing machine. The forme stayed on the base of the press, or bed, which was then moved, by steam power, towards and away from the sheet of paper it was printing. This meant that sheets of paper could be put in place and removed without interruption. Two steam-driven cylinders, taking the place of the top block, pressed the paper on to the type and a roller spread ink on the type, doing away with the slow and messy business of inking by hand with leather pads. The machine needed only two men to operate it – one to feed in the blank paper and the other to take the printed sheets away.

The steam presses were installed at *The Times* – or rather, in a building close by – in great secrecy. They were a threat to printers' jobs, and John Walter feared that if his men got to hear of his plans they would wreck the machines. He had good cause to be worried. His own newspaper had printed stories of hand-loom weavers who had

Libraries were originally private collections of books owned by a monastery or by an individual person. The big national libraries such as the Bibliotheque Nationale in France and the British Library grew out of royal book collections. These, with the Library of Congress in the United States which was begun in 1800, are the largest libraries in the world.

rioted and smashed the new steam-powered looms that were putting them out of work.

So the men from Koenig's workshop were sworn to secrecy, and as an added precaution they were split up into small teams to work on different parts of the presses. That way, no one could get a picture of the whole scheme. The presses were taken to the building near *The Times* in pieces and assembled there by a small group of trusted workmen. Supplies of paper were secretly brought in, and November 29, 1814 was chosen as the day when the steam presses would be used for the first time.

That night, the *Times* printers waited as usual by their hand-presses for the signal from John Walter to start printing. Instead, Walter told them to wait because important war news was on the way and there would have to be changes before the presses started. He had secretly had an extra set of pages made up and smuggled them to the new press

In spite of gradually relaxing controls on printing in the nineteenth century, illegal newspapers and books still flourished. This is a German "underground" press, based in a cellar. Underground presses ran a constant risk of police raids, and often had to move at short notice to new premises.

building. While the *Times* men waited, Koenig's own staff were running off the next day's paper on the steam press at 1,100 copies per hour. This proudly announced to readers that the issue had been printed by steam, "the greatest improvement connected with printing since the discovery of the art itself."

Round and round

The output of the new steam press was impressive, but it was still held back by the need to feed sheets of paper into it one by one. In 1798 a machine for making paper in reels instead of sheets was invented in France and by 1803 reels of paper were being made in Britain. The next step was to develop a press which could take a reel of paper and print on it continuously. The first such press was invented by an American, William Bullock, in 1865, but it proved unreliable.

Once again it was *The Times* that led the way. By the 1850s the main lines making up Britain's railway network had been built, offering not only faster, more reliable newspaper delivery but also the chance of increased sales in places far away from London. What was more, in 1855 the British government ended the tax on newspapers which had been in force since 1712. Sales of *The Times* leapt from forty thousand copies a day in 1851 to seventy thousand in 1861 – and once again the presses were having difficulty in meeting the increased demand.

In 1868 *The Times* installed the first successful presses to print from reels on both sides of the paper at the same time. Instead of printing from a flat forme, the machine used "stereotypes" – metal plates cast from the type. The curved plates were fitted on to rollers in the press. Once the press was started, it printed continuously, producing a reel of printed paper which was then cut and folded. The rotary press, as it was called, was to become the standard newspaper machine for over one hundred years. The only major change in that time was the replacement of steam by electric power.

Above: Early printing attempts used many more processes than those of today. Here, nine printings in different stages were used to produce a full effect.

Below: Printing found many uses – this 1892 advertising calendar illustrates the use of gas in the home.

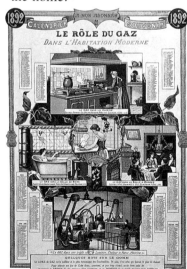

The composing room of a nineteenth century printworks. Mechanical typesetting did away with scenes like this.

Typesetting by machine

However fast the presses turned out printed copies, the most time-consuming part of the printing process was typesetting by hand and the demand for more books and papers was increasing. This was particularly annoying for newspaper publishers, who could print only as much late news as their typesetters could handle, but all printers fretted at the time and cost of hand typesetting. A skilled compositor could set about one thousand characters per hour – but a full-length book or a newspaper could contain hundreds of thousands of characters.

A problem that came up again and again was the difficulty of making a machine that would "justify" – that is, produce lines of type to an even length. The hand-compositor did this by adding thin pieces of metal between words and letters until the line was full, and sometimes by splitting long words between lines with the use of a hyphen. But this was a matter of judgment, and machines could not be taught to think.

The breakthrough came in 1886, this time in the United States. Ottmar Mergenthaler was a German watchmaker who had emigrated to the United States. After eight years' work, Mergenthaler demonstrated his own machine to a group of American newspaper owners in the summer of 1886. What he had done was to produce a mechanized version of the Gutenberg method of typesetting.

The operator used a keyboard to assemble a line of type matrices into which molten metal was poured. This produced a strip of metal type called a "slug", automatically adjusted to the length the operator had chosen in advance. The slugs were removed when enough had been cast, and transferred to the forme. When the slugs had been used the metal was melted down and returned to the machine to be used again. Meanwhile, the matrices were carried back to their store, where they were automatically sorted and stored ready for use again.

Mergenthaler's machine, christened the Linotype, was the first of a number of similar machines which were to be used in newspaper offices until the early 1980s.

Letter by letter

But Mergenthaler was not alone in working on a typesetting machine. Also in the United States, there was an amateur inventor who was thinking along similar lines. His name was Tolbert Lanston and he was a clerk in the US government offices. Lanston became interested in mechanical typesetting after he had seen a calculating machine which used cards with holes punched in them to control electrical circuits. He wondered if punched cards could be used to select matrices to cast type.

The machine he produced, after much experimentation, was called the Monotype. It was really two machines. The operator sat at a keyboard and tapped out the characters to be set. The keyboard produced a strip of paper tape with holes punched in it – a different arrangement of holes for each character. The tape was then put into a caster. The arrangement of holes determined the position of a small case containing matrices from which individual types were cast and placed in a line.

It was a race between Mergenthaler and Lanston to perfect their machines and put them on sale. Mergenthaler won by a year – but in the end it did not matter. The Linotype was faster, and ideally suited for newspaper work, but the type it produced was not very good to look at. This did not worry newspaper readers, who were more interested in reading the latest news – and the paper was thrown away at the end of the day. But people expected books to be pleasing in appearance as well as interesting to read, and the Monotype produced type which was much more attractive. So there was room for both machines – the Linotype for speed and the Monotype for quality.

But despite this steady stream of improvements, until the middle of the twentieth century the method of producing type was basically the same as Gutenberg's – pouring hot metal into the matrix of the character to be cast. And although a stereotype, or metal plate of the type, was often made from the type in the forme, typesetting in a way that Gutenberg would have recognized was still the start of the printing process. Then, quite

The Monotype casting machine came on to the market a year after the faster Linotype, but it quickly took the lead for work where the appearance of the type mattered. It cast individual letters instead of a whole line of type. Many new typefaces were specially designed for use in Monotype machines.

suddenly, there was another revolution, sparked off by the combination of computers and photography.

Lithography

Soon after World War II a new method of typesetting was introduced. It involved a photographic method of creating images of letters on film by projecting beams of light through letter shapes. This way of creating type was ideal for the method of printing called "lithography".

Lithography was a different way of printing. Gutenberg printed from letters which stood up, or were raised in "relief". The printing surface with this method was completely flat; the letters did not stand up from the surface. The printing surface, or "plate", was made by exposing the letters, through film, onto it photographically.

Lithographic machines were much faster than the old letterpress ones which used metal type. But

Rotary presses which print from curved plates on cylinders on to a continuous reel of paper. This enables high speeds to be achieved. Rotary presses were first used for newspaper work printing in black only, but later developments produced high quality results in many different shades, suitable for magazines and books. Above, the four separate pieces of film – yellow, cyan (blue), magenta and black – which are brought together for the final printing.

setting type photographically was very expensive at first, often because errors could not be spotted until the film with the letters on it had been exposed. This created difficulties when trying to correct them and frequently involved re-setting the letters. This problem was solved in the 1960s when computers were introduced into the methods.

The letters appeared on the computer screen and errors could then be seen and corrected before the film of the page was exposed. The computer also carried out many other tasks like changing the design or size of the type very quickly. It was also capable of storing vast amounts of recorded information which could be recalled onto the screen at will. The greatly increased speed made possible by the computer meant that projecting letters photographically became too slow.

Laser beams

Projecting letters has now been replaced by "digitization". Letters are turned into a code which is sent by laser beams onto film. This method means that many millions of letters can be exposed every hour, which is an enormous increase from the days of metal setting. Recent advances have meant that certain pictures can go through the same process and be included on the page along with the words at the same time.

Because all the letters, pictures, spaces and page design is now in electronic form it can be sent anywhere in the world and may even be bounced off satellites.

This has changed the whole face of printing and publishing. It is no longer necessary for everyone concerned to be working together under the same roof. Work may be done on the same publication, at the same time, all over the world. Many of our daily papers are created and printed in several cities at the same time.

Computerized typesetting, laser beams and high speed lithographic printing machines have meant that the methods concerned with making books as invented by Gutenberg have finally passed into history. Almost all newspapers and magazines, and

"Just as the invention of writing in early times had helped to 'fix' language in certain ways, spreading common words and ways of using them, so printing further advanced this process. Spellings became more standardized, local words tended to survive only in speech, while printed language increasingly tended to be used over wide areas formerly separated by dialects and local idioms."

J.M. Roberts, from "An Illustrated World History".

most books, are printed today by these new methods. The kind of printing that Gutenberg invented is most likely to be found at a small jobbing printers, or at a press that specializes in small numbers of beautifully-printed (and expensive) books.

Reading explosion!

When Gutenberg's forty-two-line Bible was printed, there were probably only a few thousand people in the whole of Europe who could read. Most of them were monks and priests. People learned new skills by watching someone else at work. They were sometimes entertained by storytellers who had learned their stories by word of mouth from someone else, or had made them up. News was spread by gossip.

Printing changed all that. Apart from religious and political books, educational texts were among the first to be printed in large numbers. Steadily, the range of books became wider. In the first half of the eighteenth century, the first books intended for the *amusement*, rather than the instruction, of children were published. At the same time, the first novels – fiction for adults – appeared.

At first, novels were about the rich, and their stories and characters were of little interest to most people. But in 1837 Charles Dickens wrote *Oliver*

Books for pleasure, books for study, books to tell you how to look after your garden or your pet, recipe books, books of poetry.... Whatever your interest, there are sure to be books about it.

57

For about five hundred years after Johann Gutenberg's death, basic methods of printing remained almost unchanged. But twentieth-century technology, including the use of computers and lasers, has greatly speeded up the production and improved the quality of print. Above, an electronic scanner separates the different films of an original so that they can be etched on to separate plates for printing. Right, quality control is still as vital.

Twist, his first big success. This story about an orphan boy's adventures, set mainly in the streets of London, had a theme and characters that everyone could sympathize with. It was the first of a long series of Dickens novels which laid bare the cruelty and suffering that many people suffered in their everyday lives.

In the United States, Mrs. Harriet Beecher Stowe achieved a similar result with *Uncle Tom's Cabin,* her novel published in 1852 which exposed the plight of black slaves.

These books, and many others like them, were read all over the world. *Uncle Tom's Cabin* was translated into over twenty languages and became a powerful weapon for the opponents of slavery. Long before the cinema and television provided a

Computer technology enables an artist to try out different images on a screen until a suitable one is created. This can then be printed and used as the basis of a book illustration. With computer graphics illustrations can be increasingly complex and visually exciting.

> *"Books are the legacies that a great genius leaves to mankind, which are delivered down from generation to generation, as presents to the posterity to those who are yet unborn."*
>
> Joseph Addison, poet, essayist and dramatist.

> *"Certain books have exerted a profound influence on history, culture, civilization and scientific thought throughout recorded time.... In every historical era, we find overwhelming evidence of the power of the written word, without which a high state of civilization and culture is inconceivable in any time or place."*
>
> Robert B. Downs, from "Books That Changed The World".

"window on the world", books were performing the same function.

Opportunity

With the spread of education in the nineteenth century, reading for pleasure became ever more popular – and possible. There was greater opportunity for people to read as well. Books and magazines and newspapers whiled away the time on rail journeys, and bookstalls became a feature of all important railway stations. Once gas and later electric lighting became common in the home, reading became less of an eye-strain. Publishers brought out editions of classics and popular novels – at very low prices – to feed the reading public's increasing appetite. Others produced self-education books so that those who had missed out at school or college could learn about subjects of interest to them or that would further them in their careers.

The increase in the availability of printed material made knowledge much more accessible. Every individual who can read now has the chance to read any kind of book, magazine or newspaper, where before it had been confined to the highly educated or church officials.

If Johann Gutenberg had never lived, someone else, sooner or later, would have hit upon the idea of printing from movable type. It is known that a number of other people, during his lifetime, were thinking on the same lines. It is even possible that someone else found the solution first, but lacked the money, skill or perseverance to carry on. Gutenberg never achieved the riches he may have hoped for, and in his lifetime he did not receive proper recognition for what he had done.

Today, new methods have taken over the printing world. But it was Gutenberg's determination over twenty years that brought print to the world. Gutenberg faced the usual disappointments and false hopes that every inventor has to deal with but he also continued to work with added debt problems. Ironically, it is these financial records that have enabled us to give credit to Gutenberg. He opened the door to freedom of knowledge for us all.

Important Dates

1398   The probable year of Johann Gutenberg's birth in Mainz, Germany.

1428   After the death of his father, Gutenberg moves from Mainz to Strasbourg.

1438   Gutenberg enters into a partnership agreement with Hans Riffe, Andres Heilmann and Andres Dritzehen to develop a secret process he has invented. Dritzehen dies the same year.

1442   The possible date of the first printed example with Gutenberg's type, a scrap of paper with eleven lines printed on it.

1443   The partnership with Riffe and Heilmann ends.

1448   Gutenberg returns to Mainz.

1450   Gutenberg meets Johann Fust and obtains a large loan from him.

1452   Fust lends more money to Gutenberg. Printing of the forty-two line Bible may have been started during this year.

1455   Fust sues Gutenberg for the return of his money, and takes over the business when Gutenberg cannot repay. Probable year of publication of the forty-two line Bible.

1456   August 24: Forty-two line Bible is known to have been published at least some weeks before this date.

1457   Fust and Schoeffer print their first book, a book of the Psalms.

1464   Following the spread of printing from Germany the first Italian printing press, run by two Germans, starts work near Rome.

1468   Gutenberg dies, aged approximately seventy.

1469   John of Speier, a German printer, sets up a press in Venice.

1470   The first printing press is set up in France followed by the Netherlands, Switzerland and Spain.

1476   William Caxton sets up the first press in England and begins printing books for entertainment. *The Cologne Chronicle* is published which contains the first acknowledgement of Gutenberg as the inventor of movable type.

1529   The English bishops publish a list of banned books.

1539   Jesuit priests introduce printing to Mexico.

1546   The Pope orders that all books about religion must be approved by the Church.

1638   The first North American printing press is set up in Cambridge, Massachusetts.

1702   The first daily newspaper, *The Daily Courant*, is published in London.

1703   The first Russian newspaper, *Vedomosti*, appears in St. Petersburg. It is run by the government.

1704   The first American newspaper, *The Boston News-Letter*, appears.

1777   France's first daily newspaper, *Le Journal de Paris*, appears for the first time.

1785   The first issue of *The Daily Universal Register,* later renamed *The Times,* is published in London.

1803   The Town Library opens at Salisbury, Connecticut, USA – the first public library in the world.

1814   November 29: *The Times* is printed for the first time on Koenig's steam press.

1820   The first books already bound are published. Previously, buyers had to arrange for their own binding.

1848   December 29: *The Times* uses a rotary press for the first time, but it proves to be unreliable.

1858   *The Times* becomes the first newspaper to be printed from stereotypes.

1868   The first successful use of reel-fed rotary presses which prints on both sides of the paper at the same time is achieved.

1886   Ottmar Mergenthaler demonstrates the first Linotype machine to American newspaper owners at the office of the *New York Tribune.*

1887   Tolbert Lanston demonstrates his Monotype typesetting machine for the first time.

1890   The first books with dust-jackets are published.

1982   *The Times* becomes the first national newspaper to be set entirely by photographic typesetting.

Printing Terms

Align: To place or set *type* so that each *character* is precisely in line with the next.

Baskerville, John: (1706-1775) An English printer to the University of Cambridge, who designed the typeface that bears his name.

Blanks: Pieces of *type* for the spaces between words.

Broadsides: A popular form of cheaply printed song and tune sheets, sold from about 1650.

Case: The place where each piece of *type* was stored before use.

Caslon, William: (1692-1766) An English typefounder whose name is attributed to the design made in his foundry.

Cast: To make *type* from molten metal using the appropriate *matrix*.

Chapbooks: Small, cheap paper-covered booklets sold in the streets.

Character: Each piece of *type*, whether a letter or punctuation mark.

Compositor: Person who sets *type* by hand into a *stick*, or by machine.

Corrupt: When a manuscript is incorrectly copied by hand so that omissions or additions appear.

Die: An engraving for the casting of *type*.

Forme: A page of *type* which has been made secure in a frame and is ready for printing.

Fount: (pronounced font) A set of matching *type* designed to fit together.

Galley: The tray in which lines of *type* were stored while the *compositor* set a whole page.

Illuminate: To decorate the pages of a book with ink, by hand.

Justify: To adjust a line of *type* to fit a space evenly with no ragged line-ends.

Lowercase: Non-capital letters, so called because of where they were stored in the *case*.

Matrix: The receptacle for the molten metal which formed the letter part of the *type*.

Rotary press: A printing press that prints on reels of paper from *stereotypes* fitted to rollers.

Stereotypes: Metal plates used for printing, made by casting from *formes* of *type*.

Stick: The hand-held device into which each piece of *type* was placed by the *compositor*. Each single line of text was made up in the *stick*.

Type: A piece of metal with a raised letter on its upper surface.

Uppercase: Capital letters, named because of the position they were stored in the *case*.

Vellum: Stretched animal skin that was used for writing on.

Woodcut: The earliest form of book illustration. Simple pictures were drawn on the end grain of blocks of hardwood and parts which were to appear white were carved away.

Index